BEYOND CLIP ART

SUNDAY SAMPLER II

· FINDING PEACE ·

WRITTEN AND ILLUSTRATED BY SHAUNA MOONEY KAWASAKI

Deseret Book Company
Salt Lake City, Utah

To Megan and Ethan

Deseret Book is a registered trademark of Deseret Book Company.
ISBN 0-87579-814-4
Printed in the United States of America
10   9   8   7   6   5   4   3   2   1

CONTENTS

Old Testament Leaders

FOREWORD

This book of illustrations is designed to be used and reused by Primary and Sunday School teachers, church leaders, students, parents, and most of all, children.

The illustrations are interchangeable and make an endless combination of visual aids. They are designed to work directly with gospel principles, the themes of peace and repentance, and the Old and New Testaments. Dual illustrations may also be used to present the concepts of right/wrong and positive/negative as well as latter-day approaches to the teachings of Jesus found in the New Testament. This material can be applied to almost any lesson or wherever a visual aid is needed to clarify the concept.

Suggested scriptures and scriptural references are given with many of the pictures. This is an aid to supplement lessons, music, or activities. We suggest that the entire contents of this book be studied and reviewed to see what is available.

HOW TO USE THIS BOOK

The visuals in this book may be enlarged or reduced on a photocopier and used in a variety of sizes and situations. The original size is an ideal, standard size for giving talks, sharing presentations, coloring pages, and accomplishing other activities. When not in use, the illustrations may be stored in 9" x 12" envelopes.

Colored pencils, crayons, or markers can be used to color the pictures. To help preserve the picture after coloring, mount it on sturdy paper. A scripture or title of the picture can be written on the back for reference. Be sure the lettering is large enough so a child can read it. Laminate the picture by covering both sides with clear contact paper. Put the picture in a labeled envelope and file for future use.

The following list offers a variety of ways the visual aids can be used. These suggestions can be altered to accommodate each class, depending on age, culture, needs, etc.

For more ideas on additional activities, games, and projects, see the original *Sunday Sampler.*

FLASH CARDS

Select pictures from the Ten Commandments in section one, from the Old Testament Stories in section three, or from the stories of Jesus in section four. Copy, color, and mount each scene on a single sheet of sturdy paper. Flash each scene to the students. Then, either have them raise their hands and tell how each situation can bring us peace, or have them search their scriptures for the reference.

GUESS ABOUT JESUS

Reduce and color all of the pictures of Jesus in section four. As the children come into the room, pin one of the pictures on the back of each child. They may ask each other "yes" and "no" questions about the pictures on their backs until they guess the story or situation. When they identify the illustration correctly, remove the picture and hang it up for everyone to see.

JESUS SAYS . . .

Copy and color the 13 latter-day pictures in section four. Tape a picture of Jesus to the wall and give the other pictures to the children (if there aren't enough children, some may hold two or more). Each picture is an example of Christlike qualities. Keep a list of these characteristics on a piece of paper to refer to. Play this game by saying to the children, "Jesus says to share the gospel" (or "be kind" or "love others"). The child holding the sharing picture brings it to the front of the room to put on display. Continue calling out "Jesus says . . ." until all of the pictures are brought to the front of the room. Talk about how peaceful and happy we feel when we do the things Jesus says.

MUSICAL CHAIRS

Copy and color enough Old Testament pictures on pages 129–171 for each child in the group. Arrange enough chairs for each child in a circle around the room. Move one of the chairs to the middle of the room. Tape the pictures on the front of the chairs. Play music while the children walk quietly around the circle of chairs. When the music stops, the music, each child will reverently find a place to sit in the circle of chairs. The standing child will then sit in the middle chair and tell about the picture on that chair. Continue the game until all the chairs are in the middle and all the children have had a chance to tell about the pictures on their chairs.

TIC-TAC-TOE

Copy and color nine negative action pictures and nine positive action pictures from sections one and two. Tape the negative pictures on the wall or blackboard in tic-tac-toe format, three across and three down. Pass out the nine positive action pictures to the children. Ask a question about each of the negative pictures and let the child with the corresponding positive picture come forward to tape it over the negative one. Play tic-tac-toe and then black out the pictures on the wall or blackboard. Talk about how we can repent, change our negative behavior, and replace it with positive behavior.

WARM AND COOL

Copy and color six or more positive pictures about peace that pertain to the lesson. Hang the pictures around the room. Choose two children to come to the front of the room. Ask the first child to describe a picture he or she has chosen. The second child then tries to find it by listening to the description. When the second child comes close to the picture, the first child says "warm," but if the second child moves away, the first child says "cool." Continue with these hints until the second child finds the correct picture. Talk about how we get warm and peaceful feelings by choosing to obey.

PUZZLE

Copy, color, and mount on sturdy paper a positive action picture and a negative action picture. Cut the negative action picture into puzzle pieces. Put the puzzle together and lay it on top of the positive action picture. Remove the pieces of the puzzle one at a time and tell the children how choosing good actions over bad actions will help us find peace.

COLORING PAGE

To support principles being taught in a lesson, copy pictures for children to color.

FATHER'S DAY CARD

Reduce and copy page 63. Glue it to the right half of an 8 1/2" x 11" piece of paper, making enough copies for all of the students. Fold the paper in half. Have the children color the picture and write a note to their father inside.

FIND A PICTURE

Reduce, copy, and color different positive and negative pictures from sections one and two that have to do with the lesson or theme. Fold the pictures in fourths and put them in a neutral colored bag. Have a child choose a picture from the bag and tell about the situation and how it might relate to real lives. When the child is finished, have him or her put the picture in one of two containers you have provided: a white container for positive pictures and a dark one for the negative. Explain to the children how making good choices will bring us peaceful, light feelings, and how bad choices will bring us dark, heavy feelings.

MOTHER'S DAY BOOKLET

Reduce and copy pages 27, 63, 69, 75, 85, 109, 187, 199, 225, 227. Trim around the borders and punch holes on the side or on top.

Tie the booklet together with yarn. Extra blank pages can be inserted. Have the children draw or color things they can do for mother on her special day or any other day.

OPPOSITES

Copy and color the negative and positive pictures in sections one and two. Hold up the negative picture in front of the group and have a volunteer tell how the child in the picture is not making a good choice and what he or she should do to make it right. Show the positive picture and talk about how making good choices helps us find peace.

POSITIVE AND NEGATIVE

Copy and color selected pairs of positive and negative pictures in sections one and two. Cut out along the borders and glue each positive and negative pair of pictures back to back. Have a child tell a story about the negative picture, turn the picture over, and then retell the same story using the positive ending. Teach the children how making positive choices makes us feel happy and peaceful.

TEN COMMANDMENTS

Copy and color the twenty pictures in section one about the Ten Commandments, pages 9–47. Fold and tape ten of the pictures (one pertaining to each commandment) underneath ten of the children's chairs. Post the remaining pictures on the board in front of the room. Tell the children how Heavenly Father gave us commandments to bring us peace and to keep us safe, then have the children find the pictures under their chairs. Ask each child to come to the front of the room and match his or her picture with another picture about the same commandment. Then ask them to put the pictures in the order in which the commandments are given in the Old Testament. Talk about each commandment and how it will bring us peace and safety.

WHAT IF—

To help the children think about consequences, copy and color several pictures pertaining to the stories in the lesson. Display the pictures and ask "What if" questions about the decisions the people are making, such as "What if the ten lepers hadn't gone to see the priests?" or "What if Esau had stayed mad at Jacob?."

WHAT IS MISSING?

Copy and color a series of pictures needed for your lesson, e.g.: animals, pages 137–143; Old Testament leaders, pages 173–177; pictures of Jesus, section four. Tape the pictures on the wall or blackboard or put them on a flannel board. Have the children close their eyes tightly. While they are not looking, remove one of the pictures. Then have the children open their eyes and guess which one is missing. Continue until the board is cleared. Stress the point that cheating is as dishonest as lying or stealing, and if anyone does cheat, the game will end.

OBEYING THE LORD'S COMMANDMENTS

1   THOU SHALT HAVE NO OTHER GODS BEFORE ME.

We should never pray to any object or person except Heavenly Father

in Jesus' name.

1   THOU SHALT HAVE NO OTHER GODS BEFORE ME.

We should always pray to our Heavenly Father who loves us.

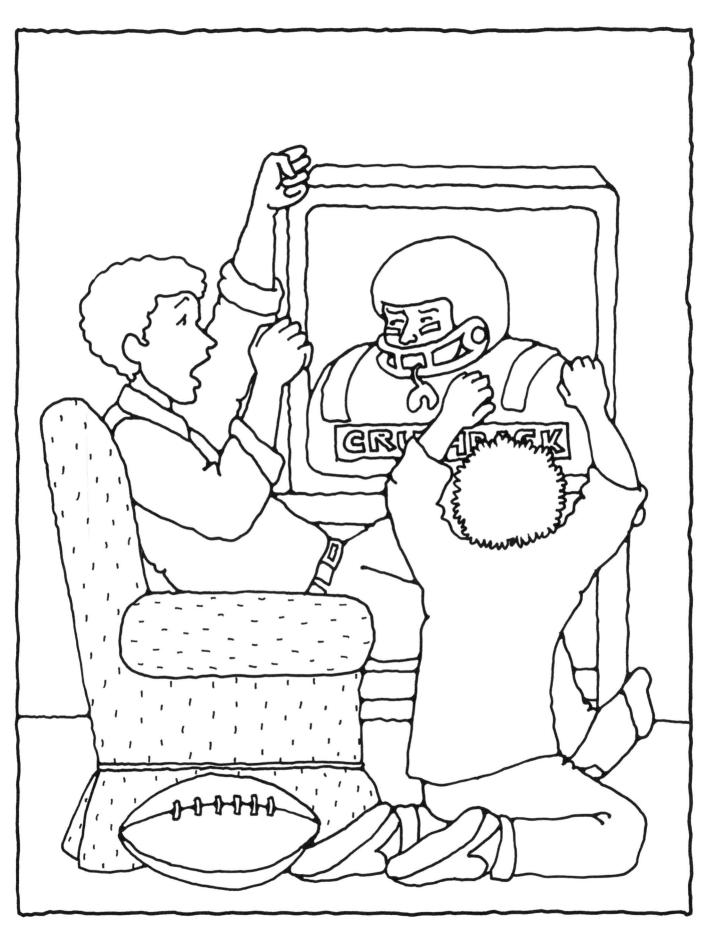

2   THOU SHALT NOT MAKE UNTO THEE ANY GRAVEN IMAGE.

We should never let other people or things take the place

of Heavenly Father and Jesus.

13

2   THOU SHALT NOT MAKE UNTO THEE ANY GRAVEN IMAGE.

We should always seek to have Heavenly Father and Jesus near us.   15

3   THOU SHALT NOT TAKE THE NAME OF THE LORD THY GOD IN VAIN.

We should never use Heavenly Father's and Jesus' names in a bad way.   17

3   THOU SHALT NOT TAKE THE NAME OF THE LORD THY GOD IN VAIN.

We should always think about Heavenly Father and Jesus with reverence.   19

4   REMEMBER THE SABBATH DAY, TO KEEP IT HOLY.

We should never do things on Sunday that lead us away

from Heavenly Father and Jesus.

4   REMEMBER THE SABBATH DAY, TO KEEP IT HOLY.

We should always remember that Sunday is Heavenly Father's

sacred day of peace and special activity.

5   HONOUR THY FATHER AND THY MOTHER.

We should love and honor our parents.   25

5 HONOUR THY FATHER AND THY MOTHER.

We should obey our parents when they ask us to help them.

6   THOU SHALT NOT KILL.

We should never be mean or unkind to any living thing.

6   THOU SHALT NOT KILL.

We should always respect Heavenly Father's children, creatures, and plants.   31

7   THOU SHALT NOT COMMIT ADULTERY.

We should never do things that would make our life

and marriage with others unhappy.

7   THOU SHALT NOT COMMIT ADULTERY.

We should always obey the marriage covenants.

8   THOU SHALT NOT STEAL.

We should never take anything that is not ours.

8   THOU SHALT NOT STEAL.

We should always be honest.

9   THOU SHALT NOT BEAR FALSE WITNESS AGAINST THY NEIGHBOUR.

We should never judge others or speak unkindly about anyone.   41

9   THOU SHALT NOT BEAR FALSE WITNESS AGAINST THY NEIGHBOUR.

We should always tell the truth and love everyone.

10   THOU SHALT NOT COVET THY NEIGHBOUR'S HOUSE, . . .

We should never desire to have other people's possessions.

10   THOU SHALT NOT COVET THY NEIGHBOUR'S HOUSE, . . .

We should always try to be grateful for what we have.

When we pay our tithing, the Church is able to help the missionary program.

When we pay our tithing, the Church is able to help the family history program.

When we pay our tithing, the Church is able to build temples.

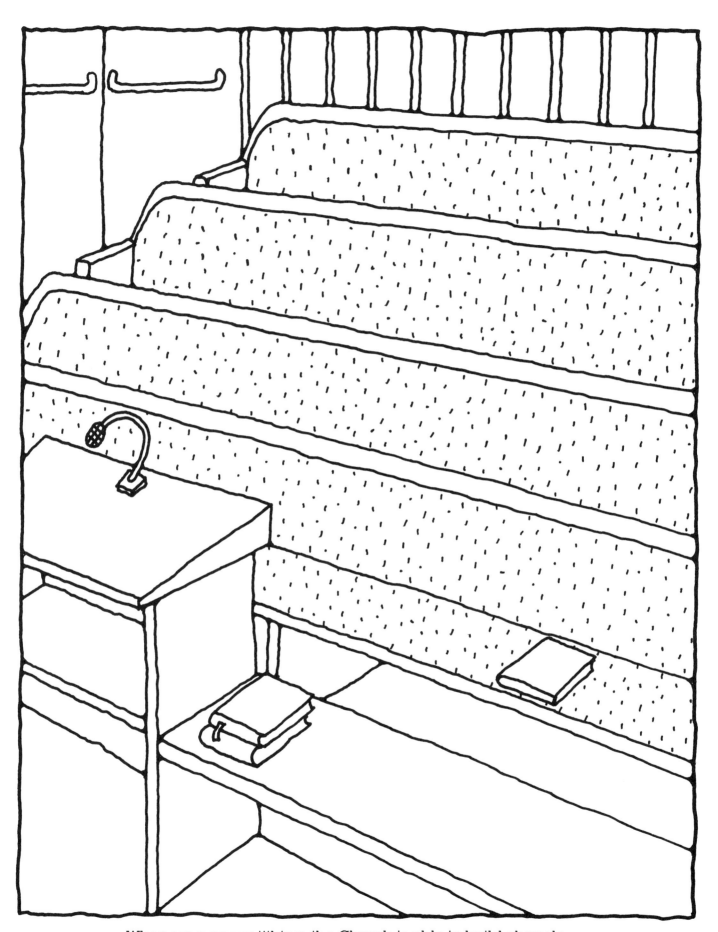

When we pay our tithing, the Church is able to build chapels.

We should never put bad things into our bodies that might harm them.

We should always eat good things to help nourish our bodies.

GIVING THANKS, FORGIVING, AND SHARING

We are thankful for our families.

We are thankful for brothers and sisters.

We are thankful for a warm home.

We are thankful for good food.

We are thankful for clean water.

We are thankful for warm clothing.

We are thankful for employment.

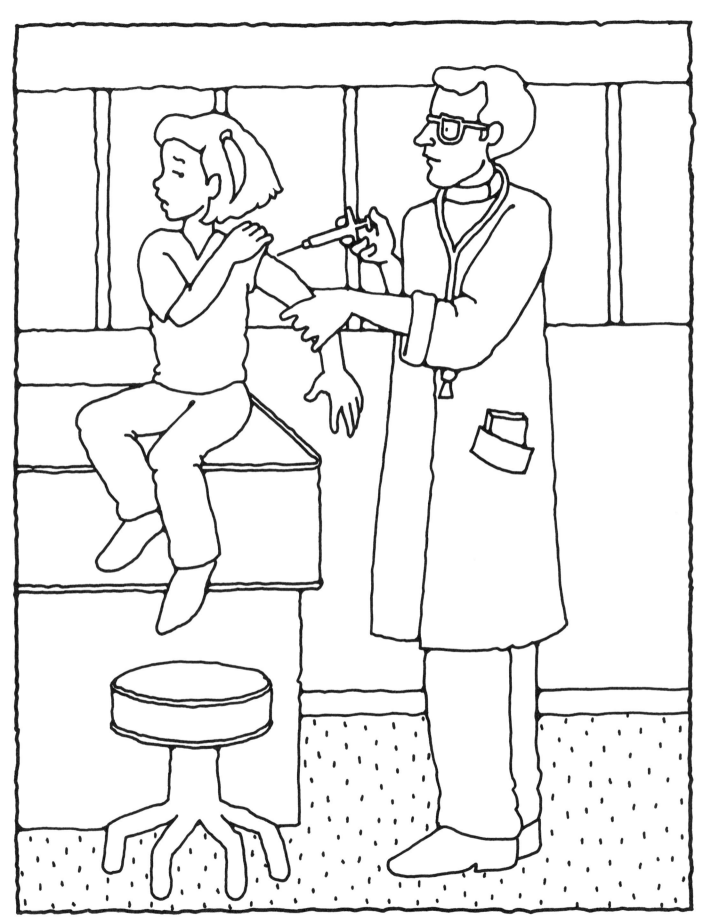

We are thankful for modern medicine.

We are thankful for modern technology.

We are thankful for the gospel and for missionary work.

Sometimes accidents happen.

We can feel peace by saying we are sorry and making things right.

We can't feel peace if we make bad choices.

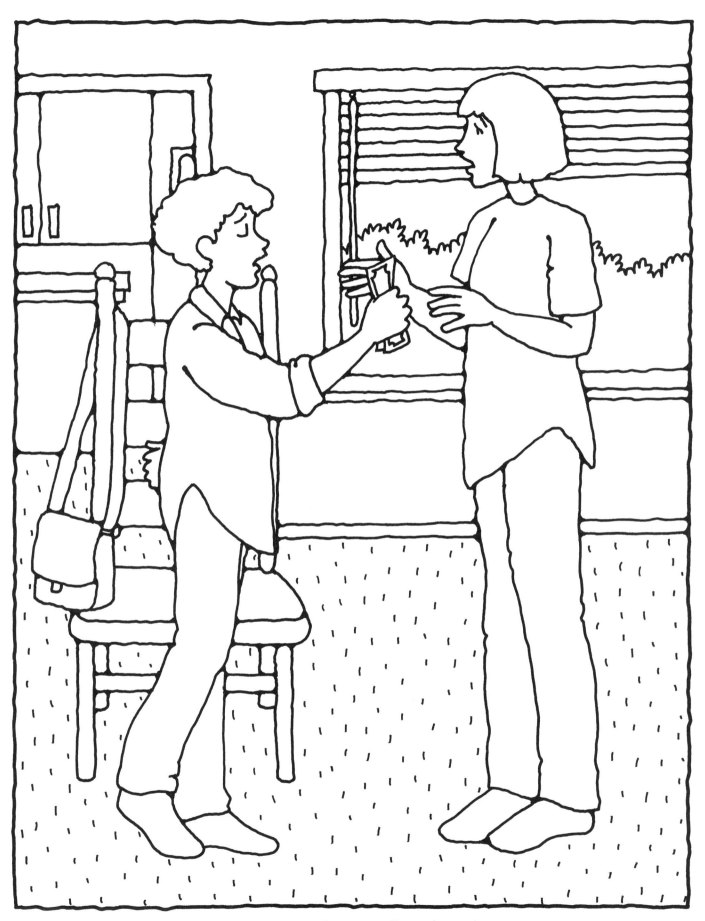

We can feel peace by repenting of our sins.

We can't feel peace if we dislike ourselves for what we do.

We can feel peace by forgiving ourselves too.

We can't feel peace if we are confused and mixed up.

We can feel peace if we talk to someone about our problems.

Sometimes grown-ups make mistakes.

We can feel peace by loving and forgiving grown-ups when it's needed.

We can't feel peace when we don't share.

We can feel peace by sharing with others.

We can't feel peace without asking before we borrow.

We can feel peace by returning the things we borrow.

We can't feel peace unless we consider others' feelings.

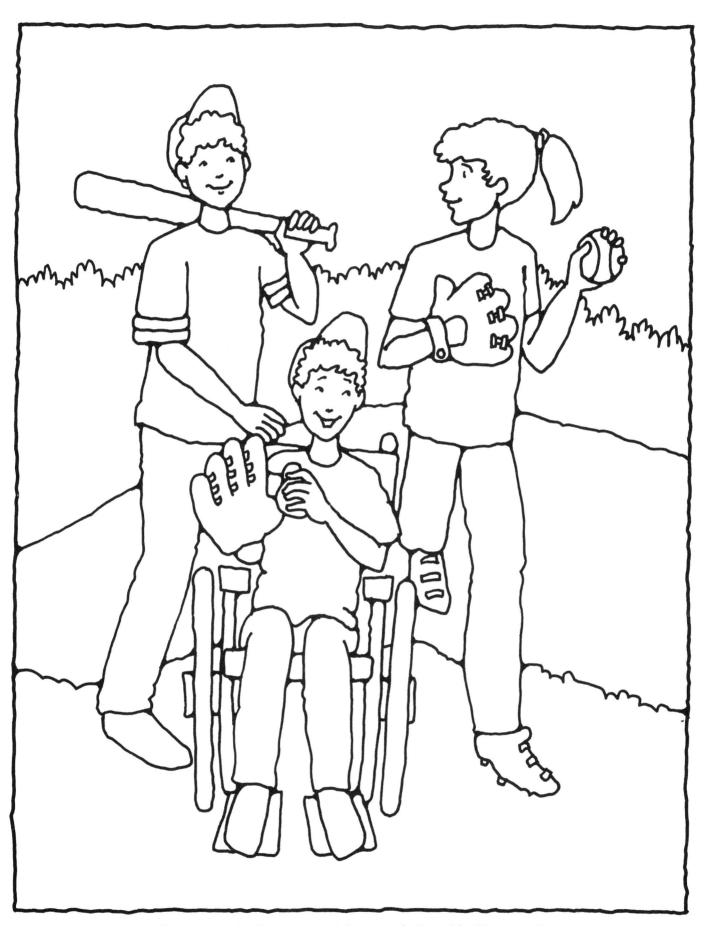

We can feel peace by being considerate of others' feelings and needs.

We can't feel peace when we leave a mess behind us.

We can feel peace if we leave an area nicer than we found it.

We can't feel peace if we fight with our brothers or sisters.

We can feel peace if we love our family members like best friends.

We can't feel peace if we don't help.

We can feel peace and love if we all do our share without being asked.

STUDYING THE
SCRIPTURES

CAIN AND ABEL

"The Lord had respect unto Abel and to his offering: But unto Cain and
to his offering he had not respect. And Cain was very wroth." (Genesis 4:4–5.)

THE CITY OF ENOCH

"Lo; Zion in process of time, was taken up into heaven.

And the Lord said unto Enoch: *Behold mine abode forever.*" (Moses 7:21.)

NOAH

"Make thee an ark of gopher wood; . . . and . . . two of every (living thing) shalt   133
thou bring into the ark, to keep them alive with thee." (Genesis 6:14, 19.)

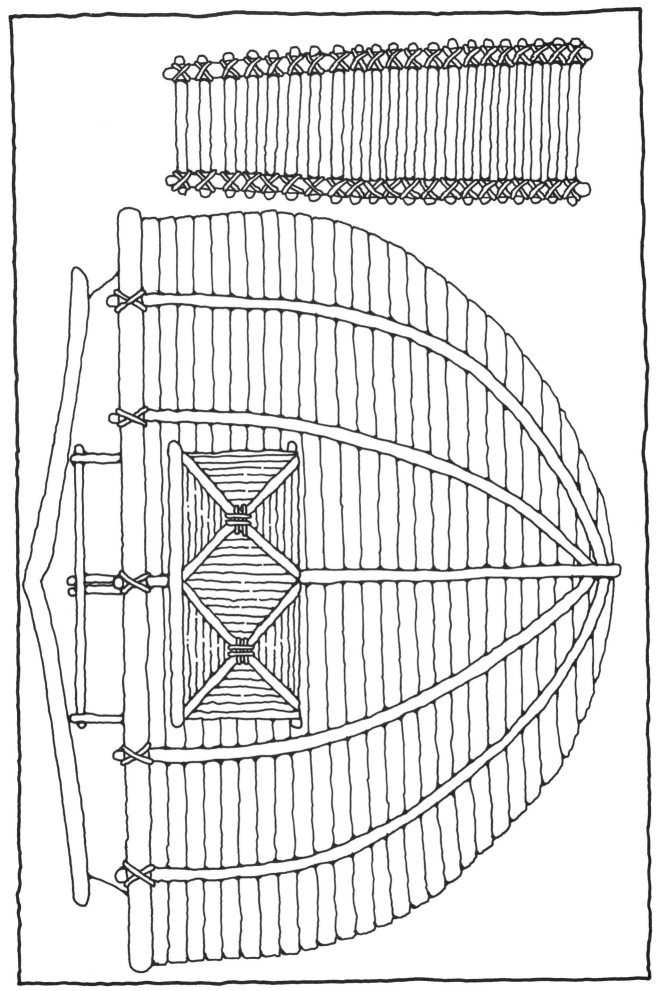

The Ark

137

The Animals

The Animals

141

The Animals

THE TOWER OF BABEL

"Let us build us a city and a tower, whose top may reach unto heaven; . . . And the

Lord said, . . . *Let us go down, and there confound their language.*" (Genesis 11:4, 6–7.)

ABRAHAM AND THE THREE HOLY MEN

"And the men rose up from thence, and looked toward Sodom:

and Abraham went with them to bring them on the way." (Genesis 18:16.)

LOT AND HIS FAMILY

"(The angel of the Lord) said, . . . *Look not behind thee . . . lest thou be consumed. . . .*   149
But (Lot's) wife looked back . . . and she became a pillar of salt." (Genesis 19:17, 26.)

HAGAR AND ISHMAEL

"And the angel of God called to Hagar, . . . *Arise, lift up the lad, and hold him*   151

in thine hand; for I will make him a great nation." (Genesis 21:17–18.)

ESAU AND JACOB (ISRAEL)

"Esau said to Jacob, *Feed me . . . for I am faint. . . .* Jacob said, *Sell me . . . thy birth-right. And Esau said, . . . what profit shall this birthright do to me?*" (Genesis 25:30–32.)

153

THE EGYPTIANS

"And the waters returned, and covered the chariots, and the horsemen, and all the host of Pharaoh that came into the sea after them." (Exodus 14:28.)

MOSES

"And the Lord said unto Moses, . . . *thou shalt smite the rock,*

and there shall come water out of it, that the people may drink." (Exodus 17:5–6.)

157

BALAAM AND THE ANGEL OF THE LORD

"The Lord opened the eyes of Balaam, and he saw the angel of the Lord
standing in the way, and his sword drawn in his hand." (Numbers 22:31.)

159

GIDEON AND HIS ARMY

"And the Lord said unto Gideon, *By the three hundred men that lapped*
will I save you, and deliver the Midianites into thine hand." (Judges 7:7.)

161

ELIJAH AND THE PROPHETS OF BAAL

"Elijah challenges the prophets of Baal to call down fire from heaven—They fail—   163
He calls down fire (and) slays the prophets of Baal." (1 Kings 18.)

ELIJAH AND ELISHA

"Behold, there appeared a chariot of fire, and horses of fire, and parted them both 165
asunder; and Elijah went up by a whirlwind into heaven." (2 Kings 2:11.)

JOB

"And the Lord said unto Satan, *Hast thou considered my servant Job, that there is none like him in the earth, . . . one that feareth God, and escheweth evil?*" (Job 1:8.)

EZEKIEL

"As I was among the captives by the river of Chebar, . . .
the heavens were opened, and I saw visions of God." (Ezekiel 1:1.)

169

DANIEL AND KING NEBUCHADNEZZAR

"Then Arioch brought in Daniel before the king in haste, and said . . . , *I have found a* 171
man . . . that will make known unto the king the (dream's) interpretation." (Daniel 2:25.)

Adam   Eve   Seth   Enoch   Methuselah   Noah

Shem   Abraham   Sarah   Isaac   Jacob   173

Joseph   Moses   Ruth   Saul   David

Solomon   Elijah   Elisha   Hezekiah   Nehemiah 175

Esther   Isaiah   Jeremiah   Ezekiel   Daniel

Amos   Jonah   Micah   Zechariah   Malachi   177

HELPING AND SERVING OTHERS

JESUS CALMS THE TEMPEST

"There arose a great storm of wind, . . . And (Jesus) said . . . *Peace, be still.* . . . And he   181
said unto (the disciples), *Why are ye so fearful . . . (and) have no faith?*" (Mark 4:37–40.)

I will find peace if I have faith in Jesus Christ.

JESUS OVERCOMES TEMPTATION

"And (Jesus) was there in the wilderness forty days, tempted of Satan; and   185

was with the wild beasts; and the angels ministered unto him." (Mark 1:13.)

I will find peace if I fast, pray, and resist temptation as Jesus did.

JESUS ESTEEMS THE WIDOW AND HER OFFERING

"(Jesus) . . . saw the rich men casting their gifts into the treasury. . . .

And he said, . . . *This poor widow hath cast in more than they all.*" (Luke 21:1–3.)

189

I will find peace if I give as Jesus taught us to do.

JESUS MENDS THE EAR OF THE SERVANT

"And one of them . . . cut off (the servant's) right ear. And Jesus answered and said,   193

Suffer ye thus far. And he touched his ear, and healed him." (Luke 22:50–51.)

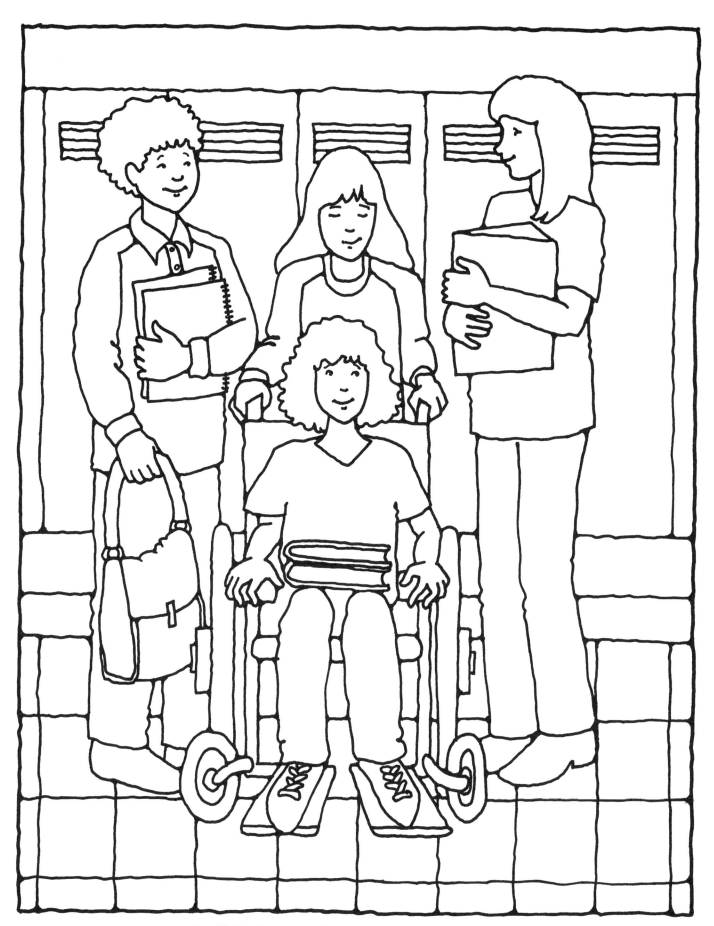

I will find peace if I serve others as Jesus did.

JESUS COUNSELS THE RICH YOUNG RULER

"(Jesus) said, . . . *It is easier for a camel to go through a needle's eye,*
than for a rich man to enter into the kingdom of God." (Luke 18:24–25.)

I will find peace if I live and find happiness as Jesus did.

JESUS SEEKS OUT THE DESPISED ZACCHAEUS

"And when Jesus came to the (tree where Zacchaeus was), he looked up, . . . and 201
said unto him, . . . *Come down; for to day I must abide at thy house.*" (Luke 19:3–5.)

I will find peace if I love others as Jesus did.

JESUS HEALS THE NOBLEMAN'S SON

"Jesus saith unto him, *Go thy way; thy son liveth.* And the man believed the word

that Jesus had spoken unto him, and he went his way." (John 4:50.)

I will find peace if I have compassion for others as Jesus did.

JESUS FORGIVES THE SINFUL WOMAN

"Wherefore I say unto thee, *Her sins, which are many, are forgiven*. . . . And   209
(Jesus) said to the woman, *Thy faith hath saved thee; go in peace.*" (Luke 7:47, 50.)

I will find peace if I forgive others as Jesus did.

JESUS FEEDS THE FIVE THOUSAND

"And (Jesus) took the five loaves, and the two fishes, and looking up to heaven, he blessed, and brake, . . . and they did all eat, and were filled." (Matthew 14:19–20.)

213

I will find peace if I share with others as Jesus did.

JESUS IS THANKED BY THE LEPER

"And one of (the lepers), when he saw that he was healed, turned back, . . .   217

and fell down on his face at (Jesus') feet, giving him thanks." (Luke 17:15–16.)

I will find peace if I express my gratitude as Jesus wants us to do.

JESUS TEACHES THE WOMAN AT THE WELL

"Jesus . . . said unto her, *Whosoever drinketh of this water shall thirst again: But whosoever drinketh of the water that I shall give him shall never thirst.*" (John 4:13–14.)

I will find peace if I share my testimony with others as Jesus did.

JESUS LOVES AND HONORS HIS MOTHER

"(The crucified Jesus) . . . saith unto his mother, *Woman, behold thy son!* . . . (and to   225
John), *Behold thy mother!* . . . (And John) took her unto his own home." (John 19:26–27.)

I will find peace if I honor my parents as Jesus did.

JESUS BRINGS THE GOSPEL TO THE NEPHITES

"Jesus . . . did minister unto the people of Nephi. . . . and he took their little children, . . .   229
and prayed unto the Father for them." (3 Nephi 11: introduction; 17:21.)

I will find peace if I share the gospel with others as Jesus did.